KT-225-897

Start Reading
AND THINKING

Bouncing with the Budgie

Celia Warren

QED Publishing

Bouncing with the Budgie

Budgie's bouncing,
Kitten's pouncing,
Dog is fast asleep.

Mum is trusting
Dad with the dusting,
Cooker's going 'Beep'!

Bouncing with the Budgie

Copyright © QED Publishing 2005

First published in the UK in 2005 by
QED Publishing
A Quarto Group company
226 City Road
London EC1V 2TT
www.qed-publishing.co.uk

All rights reserved. No part of this publication may be reproduced, stored in
a retrieval system, or transmitted in any form or by any means, electronic,
mechanical, photocopying, recording, or otherwise, without the prior permission
of the publisher, nor be otherwise circulated in any form of binding or cover other
than that in which it is published and without a similar condition being imposed
 the subsequent purchaser.

A Catalogue record for this book is available from the British Library.

ISBN 1 84538 455 5

Written by Celia Warren
Designed by Caroline Grimshaw
Editor Hannah Ray
Illustrated by Caroline Martin

Series Consultant Anne Faundez
Publisher Steve Evans
Creative Director Louise Morley
Editorial Manager Jean Coppendale

Printed and bound in China

Budgie's singing,
Telephone's ringing,
Sister's going out.

My room's tidy
And it's Friday,
So I want to **shout**:

Budgie, go on bouncing!
Kitten, give me five!
Dog, wake up and play with me!
Weekend, come alive!

5

Lots of Socks

I've got lots of socks:
long socks, short socks,
school socks, sport socks,

socks with stripes,
socks with spots,
socks all tangled up in knots,

white socks, grey socks,
everyday socks,
blue socks, red socks,
fluffy bed-socks,

socks **too big**,
socks too small,
socks I never wear at all,

socks on my feet,
socks in the drawer,
one odd sock
on the bedroom floor –

that's the sock I'm looking for!

Cake-o-saurus

Why don't we bake
a dinosaur cake
and call it Munchosaurus?

Why don't we bake
a dinosaur cake
and call it Stickisaurus?

Give it horns
of ice-cream cones
and call it Crunchosaurus.

Add gingernut eyes
and buttercream thighs
and call it Bickisaurus.

Why don't we bake
a dinosaur cake
and call it whatever we think?

Then let it cool
and eat it all
until it is extinct.

Neversaurus

When dinosaurs roamed the earth,
So huge it was easy to spot 'em,
You'd frequently see a Triceratops
But never a tricerabottom!

Butter My Bread

Butter my bread,
   Ice my cake,
      Show me a duck
         On a frozen lake.

Push my swing,
   Catch my ball,
      Show me a goose
         By a garden wall.

Button my coat,
Find my gloves,
Show me a crow
That nobody loves.

Tell me a story,
Sing me a song,
Hold my hand
And before very long

I'll butter your bread,
And ice your cake
And show you a duck
On a frozen lake.

Seagull in the Field

Seagull in the field is
Pattering its feet,
Up comes the worm,
Down goes the beak.

Seagull in the field sings,
High above the sea,
"Fish for my breakfast,
Worm for my tea!"

Through the Window

One day a worm looked through a little window
And saw a starfish, far from sea or sand,
But the window was the glass of a jam jar,
And the starfish was a small boy's hand.

Squirrel

He flies without wings.
He jumps without springs.
High in the treetops
  he chatters and sings:

      racing,
        chasing,
          squirrel.

He tiptoes on branches.
He takes lots of chances.
His tail helps him balance
  wherever he dances:

      jumping,
     bumping,
    squirrel.

14

He shakes the nuts down
when they're shiny and brown.
He nibbles them, dropping
   their shells on the ground:

                    cracking,
                         snacking,
                              squirrel.

When the Princess Broke Her Crown

Flags drooped and wouldn't flutter,
    Milk wouldn't turn to butter,
The king could only moan and mutter
    When the princess broke her crown.

Water fountains turned to ice,
    Cats refused to chase the mice,
The queen shed tears once or twice
    When the princess broke her crown.

But with paper and paint and lots of glue
    The princess made a crown, brand new,
In flamingo-pink with glittery-blue:
    A brand new paper crown.

Then, suddenly, flags flew high in the air,
    There was butter for toast and more to spare,
The king and queen said, "We don't care
    That the princess broke her crown."

The king laughed; the queen smiled
    To see their happy little child
In her crown, so carefully styled:
    Her home-made paper crown.

In the Bath

Here is a place
where I like to flop.
Here is a place
where bubbles pop.

Here is a place
where I play with my boat,
and see my toes
and fingers float.

Night Ride

When I can't sleep
I shut my door
And sit on the rug
On my bedroom floor.

I open my window,
I close my eyes
And say magic words
Till my carpet flies:

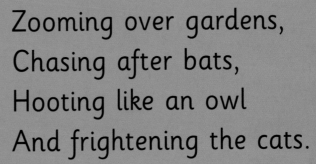

Zooming over gardens,
Chasing after bats,
Hooting like an owl
And frightening the cats.

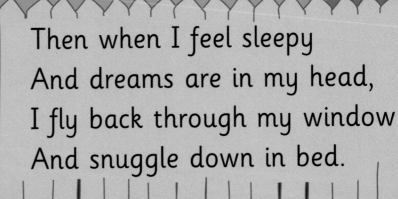

Then when I feel sleepy
And dreams are in my head,
I fly back through my window
And snuggle down in bed.

19

What do you think?

Do you know all the days of the week? Which days make the weekend?

Can you remember what the seagull had for his tea?

Do your socks match any in the 'Lots of Socks' poem?

Can you find the one, real dinosaur's name in this book?

Can you find all the rhyming words in the poem 'Squirrel'?

What do you do when you cannot sleep?

Who was upset when the princess broke her crown?

Read 'Through the Window' on page 13.
Did the worm really see a starfish?

Parents' and teachers' notes

- Read 'Lots of Socks' (pages 6–7) aloud. Re-read, omitting the rhyming words and encouraging your child to remember/guess the missing words.

- Ask your child to find all the made-up dinosaur names in 'Cake-o-saurus' (pages 8–9). Together, invent more names with an edible theme, e.g. 'chocosaurus', 'lollisaurus'.

- Provide a choice of materials and challenge your child to make a paper crown like the princess's (pages 16–17). Re-read the poem, and compare your child's crown to the princess's crown.

- Make a wall-frieze, featuring a cross-section of a house, a garden, trees, fields, a park, a frozen lake etc. Make copies of some or all of the poems in the book and let your child decide where on the frieze the different poems belong. For example, 'Squirrel' could be placed by the trees, 'Cake-o-saurus' next to the kitchen in the house, 'Butter My Bread' by the lake or the park etc.

- Ask your child to choose a favourite place in his or her home. Together, write a poem describing the chosen place in the style of 'In the Bath' (page 18). Start with 'Here is a place where …'.

- Encourage your child to move to the words of 'Butter My Bread' (pages 10–11). Try walking, running, hopping and skipping. Which action best suits the poem's rhythm? (The poem can be used as a skipping rhyme, for use with a skipping rope.)

- Find additional rhymes for each verse in 'When the Princess Broke Her Crown' (pages 16–17), e.g. 'clutter', 'dice', 'stew', 'chair'. Help your child to make up some alternative or additional lines for the poem.

- Discuss which words would need to be left out to turn the poem 'Squirrel' (pages 14–15) into a riddle. (Answer: the word 'squirrel'!)

- Read 'Through the Window' (page 13). Pretend that you and your child are looking through an imaginary window. What can you see? Encourage your child to be as imaginative as possible.

- Read 'Night Ride' (page 19). Explain to your child that the girl in the poem has not really flown out of her window on a magic carpet – she is using her imagination.

- Compare the first and last verses of 'Butter My Bread' (pages 10–11). How do the words differ?

24